Also by Jack H. Bender

Disregarded: Transforming the School and Workplace through Deep Respect and Courage

Moonflower and Other Poems I Didn't Write

Three Simple Words

Jack H. Bender

with paintings by
Cindy M. Bender

InnerWork Publications
Zeeland, Michigan

In Appreciation

I'm grateful to my family for their encouragement and for their appreciation of my work.

Thanks go to my friends at Hope Academy of Senior Professionals (HASP) who continue to demonstrate how valuable and restorative poetry is to the human soul.

Also, thanks to my readers who often say that *Moonflower* can be found on the nightstand beside their bed.

As my editor, Sara Leeland has been a superb partner: culling from the herd, grooming, grouping and finally, sending to market. Thank you, Sara.

Because *Three Simple Words* is a print-on-demand book, I am grateful to be minimizing the environmental impact of book production.

Finally, thanks to my wife Cindy who provided the cover art and all other watercolors throughout. I am delighted to include some of her work, which leaves me wondering how an empty sheet of paper can accept so much of the world's beauty.

Dedication

Three Simple Words is dedicated to those who suffer from injury, poor health or loss, which, of course, is all of us. And, especially, to my family. May even the darkest of poems contained herein offer slivers of light, hope and restoration.

Contents

Part XI: Inner Life

Part I

Hope in Community

Party!

A Sign of Human Nature (4/15/13)

A documentary need not be filmed,
nor a book written.

A statue need not be erected,
nor medals be given.

It need only be said,
that when two explosions rocked Boston,
and its beloved marathon,

exhausted runners
ran to hospitals to give blood.

The Downward Spiral Path

You are suffering.
The news stuns,
but I am a world away.

With so little to offer,
I turn to my ritual
of solidarity.

I sink into silence.
I grow sullen.
I become irritable.

Nothing satisfies.
And, then,
the pain manifests.

A mantra of you
overcomes all other thought.
I am suffering.

The fool's place
to where I have traveled
helps no one.

Yet, in love's logic,
I have crossed the span,
and hold you in my arms,

eating the bitterness
and the sadness,
until they have vanished.

And, in our darkest hour together,
I invoke the gods—
mine and yours.

Immigration

We could solve
one of our biggest challenges
by going to the movies.

After purchasing a ticket,
we could buy popcorn and Milk Duds,
and settle into our seats.

The lights would dim
and the narrator would say
that we're in Mexico.

Chickens run over the bare earth
as do hungry children,
dressed only in T-shirts.

We follow "Juan," an alias,
as he prepares to leave his family
and cross over the border.

The "coyote" demanded three years of savings
and has said so little,
that Juan must walk by faith.

Walk he does.
At night. Into the desert,
with as much water as he can carry.

He walks past a trail of clothes
others have dropped to lighten their load,
then a body.

He reaches the U.S. with no money.
No food. No lodging. No job.
He only speaks Spanish.

All this risk
is in the hopes of feeding his family.

If he's extremely lucky,
he will land a job
no one else wanted.

If he's unlucky,
he will fall prey to others,
be jailed or deported.

We will leave the theater feeling
that such desperation
must be met with uncommon compassion.

It only takes a movie
to know what to do.

There Has Never Been a Happiness

so pure
as mine last night.

Everyone that mattered was here.
Love. Laughter.

Food. Rivers of drink.
Concentrated joy.

My whole world
in the living room.

I cannot describe the harshness
that greeted me

when I fell
from that tree,

finally realizing
that more than half of them
are dead.

What now?
The cold… The warmth…
Neither will yield.

I have never been so careless
as I was at dawn.

The Poverty of Plenty

The joy of having little
has slipped through my grasp.
Now, my hands hold
the distractions of our time.

Just like the poor of the world,
I was once a child who had nothing
to hinder my joy.

Our minister stopped by
and asked if I needed shoes.

My father went to the junkyard,
came back with a box of parts
and built my first bike.

When older, I baled straw with a friend
to pay for a movie.
I loved that movie.

In our first year of marriage
our Christmas tree was a candle
atop a small step ladder.

The poor have their feet
firmly on the ground.
I hover with aching arms.

Ode to Our Humanity

"Man Drowns Saving Dog"
"Neighbor Donates Kidney"
"Policeman Killed Saving Jumper"
"Local Soldier Remembered"

The news is dark, distant,
and unable to convey
that little has been lost
and that much has been gained.

For to live the great paradox,
we must throw ourselves on need,
for the sake of stranger, and those closer still,
or we shall perish.

Profound Encounter

for K

Our meeting had ended,
so I thought we'd just wish each other good night,

but Karen approached, and squared her feet.
Even without a word from her,
I sensed that I should listen well.

"Churches, government, business…
It's…
It's such a mess!
They're all decaying…

There isn't anything big
that we can do about it,
but we can do what we can.

I barter. That keeps the threads of community alive.
If I've got it, I give it away.
If I need something, I ask for it.
It's as simple as that.

But nothing can have a price tag on it.
You can't worry about even-steven.
It's give and take, no strings attached.

If we have to start over
and rebuild everything from scratch,
maybe that's as good a place to start as any."

A New World

If we stop judging each other,
crocuses will bloom.

The Midterm Student

His face is half gone now,
but I can still see his silhouette
in the doorway.

The counselor had brought him
to my classroom,
in the middle of the term.

He had rough edges
and seemed to be
frantically treading water,

though he stood still before me.
I gave him as much time
and good will as I could—

and then he was gone.
Weeks later, I learned
that his sleeping in other people's garages

was far better than going "home"
to violence and desolation.
I was livid at the counselor

for having kept his situation secret.
But, of course, we'd been told
to treat the stranger as if the stranger were Jesus.

If that image is daunting,
we could treat the stranger
as if the stranger sleeps in a garage at night.

Thanksgiving in D.C.

One man stands out
among the people eating dinner
with all the fixings.

Bearded, ill-kept,
his bright blue eyes
dart between the volunteers
and his feast.

More turkey! he commands.
More potatoes!
More coffee!
More rolls! he yells,
with the authority of a king.

The volunteers
are obedient serfs,
and move rapidly
while displaying genuine smiles.

Sated, the king leaves,
unceremoniously,
going into the street,

into his domain,
looking for a place
to sleep for the night.

The Helmet

Two deeply tanned men
go about their work
in provided blue pants and white shirts
that are covered with today's dust.

The younger checks his wristwatch
for coffee-break time.
The other pulls a leather strap
and watch from his pocket,
to do the same.

When close to lunch
they'll repeat the ritual.
No one needs a time piece
for the work they do.

There are simple sights, sounds and rhythms
that soon go to the bone.

There is a third worker—
maybe high school age,
dressed in his own jeans
and a white T-shirt.
He wears a hard hat and gloves.

With a long-handled shovel
he cleans the small cones
from under the conveyers.

He's even more interested in the time
than the other two.

Shovel. Check time.
Shovel. Check time.

Some piles remain,
but the young man
heads for the large garage.

He enters, then reappears
with a welder's helmet and a grin.

As the light turns surreal
and the sparrows disappear,
the two men, and now another,
gather around the young man
as he puts on the helmet
and looks skyward.

The helmet is passed from one man
to the next, and around again.

The astronomers make observations
and confer among themselves
until the dump trucks come to be loaded.

On my iPhone

I read that Ghana
is outlawing the killing of babies
with birth defects.

Citizens are being told
that abnormalities
are not the work of evil spirits.

Hope

If you want to see
the face of hope,

find mothers
who scavenge for food,

gritting their teeth
and brushing away tears,

only turning soft
when their children are near.

Ignore the idle men
beneath the trees

whose hearts and legs
have turned to stone.

Hide and Seek

Oh, dear friend,
take my hand.
We will not stop
until we've found it.

We'll look beneath the stove
and in forgotten closets,
behind the couch,
on dusty shelves,

and underneath the runner.
We'll search in the garden,
behind the barn,
and out in the fields,

shouting as we go,
Humanity! Humanity!
Come out, come out,
wherever you are!

Split Opinions
for A.N.A.

They have played cribbage
in the colder months
on nearly every Monday night
for the last thirty-five years.

On this Monday, the serious one asks a question.
"Gun control…
Why do you think
people feel the need to own guns?"

Beliefs run deep and hot.
Bringing themselves back to a simmer,
measured answers come from around the table,
as if each one had played a card in turn.

"Conspiracy theories. You know —
Defend yourself from Big Brother."
Heads nod.
"Foreign invasion."
Nods again.

"To protect ourselves from each other."
Play stops…

The sportscaster on the tube says
that it's Calgary against Los Angeles tonight.
Lewis of the Kings will probably keep alive his scoring
    streak.
Los Angeles is favored, but Calgary's on fire.

"Well, probably all three," comes from the table,
making sharp teeth dull.
"Final card," is called.
A peg is moved, and totaling points begins.

Furnace
for C

During the Great Recession,
after her workplace closed,
my friend would land jobs,

but suffer lay-offs the day before a raise
or going on health insurance.
(May predators be damned to Hell!)

Then nothing.
Only living on the edge.

The joblessness
stretched into the darkness of winter—
No job. No health insurance
Bills. Mortgage. Depleting retirement fund.

The only release was to journal,
recording her grief and her prayers.
Surely, this was "bottom,"
all the way down.

With a winter storm pressing,
she prayed that the furnace
would not fail.

When its cycle ended,
she would wait in the silence,
hoping and praying that it would turn on again.

It held,
this spiritual being
who could answer prayers.

I Kept Staring

at your empty seat
for much of the day,
wondering where you were,
my heart a hollow drum.

But, then, you entered,
dressed in Sunday clothes,
walking like a scolded dog,
fixing your eyes on the creaking floor.

Something was wrong.

Mrs. Buehler was reading
a funny book to the class
with her warbling voice,
showing us the pictures
as her bulging bracelet
jangled with each page.

I kept staring.
Everyone in the class was laughing
except you, and then me.

Your hand would streak
to your mouth to stifle a laugh,
your body jerking forward
as if someone had slammed on the car brakes.

I kept staring
from two rows over,
unable to look into your eyes,
seeing you become rigid
as a steel rod.

Who died?
Were they close to you?

I kept staring,
the story fading,
the clock sleeping,
the room as quiet
as swimming underwater.

You heaved again
and a flash escaped
from around your hand.

I began to hurt for you.
You thought it the end of the world,
but those things didn't matter.

You were still pretty,
maybe the most beautiful sixth-grader
there ever was.

The Good Old Days...

I often romanticize the past,
maybe imagining a farmer,

rocking on his front porch,
contentedly watching his crops.

I know better.

Uncle John,
in from the fields for lunch,

drank his coffee
from a saucer,

there being
no time to waste.

Across Town

For J and J

a family is treading in blackest water.
No one can imagine their pain
or how they will ever reach shore.

This flood will not be bound.
It has spread all over town,

running under doors and into kitchens,
seeping into cracks
and drenching all it touches.

We know you love this family
and that their tsunami
has become your own.

And so, in kind,
the breakers crash over us.

The brine flows from our eyes
and soaks our shoes.
We've channeled ripples as far as Brazil.

You've tried to carry on
by fixing meals, ferrying children,
and swimming to work with stones in your pockets.

But you're undone,
waking up in Aisle 4
during a downpour

wondering if you drove,
or were driven.

Forgetting

After twenty and five years in prison,
the white power brokers ordered drivers
to take Mandela for short trips.

Through the car window
Mandela could see what South Africa
had become in his long absence.

Before secret talks began
about his release
and how apartheid might dissolve,

he was fitted with a suit,
and told to dress well
to meet the current officials.

After so many years of wearing prison attire
he had forgotten how to tie a tie
and tie his shoe laces.

Much had slipped through the cold bars.
But he had come to remember
how to lead millions of his people.

There Are No Two Things

called you and me—
no separation

between the swaying trees
and breath,

nor the heaving ocean
and tears.

And this shared thought
arose while the grasses grew

and the weaver
continued to weave.

Waking Late

Only now do I realize
that Jesus had spoken true,

that we can
"do greater things than these."

If only I had known…
For my part,

there would be more flowers,
fewer tears,

and love of neighbor
would reign.

The Quote that Stuck

Bob Sherwood was a good man.
Even when I was young,
he treated me well.
In his presence,
one always felt good.

When he became ill,
he had a chance
to write a letter to us all,
to be read at his funeral.

I have forgotten nearly all
of his words that were read
on that sad day.

As I think of those remaining,
I marvel at how well they fit
the turnings of our lives—
leaving home for kindergarten,
moving to college,
going off to war,
heading for surgery.

From the good man
that had lived a good life:
"I don't want to go,
but I can't stay."

This Tavern is Closing*

Friends, we have to stop meeting like this.
This tavern is closing.

But, before we part, what shall we say of our journey?

That we were moths giving in to the light?
That we longed for wine that would keep us drunk?
Or that we learned to love in countless ways?

That we travelled through time in a wobbly boat—
across the sea and over mountains—to reach a garden?

That we left our old houses, knowing we couldn't return?
That love's knife entered our hearts?
Or that we jumped in a basket and built a road to God?

That we begged to die and so to grow?
That we scorned rules of *this* world, but refused to be jailed?

Perhaps we have talked too much.
Perhaps it is enough to say, that, to shed light on the path,
we set ourselves on fire.

Perhaps silence or a flute melody would be better by far.

* Created for the last session of a HASP poetry class

Considering My Coffee

The outside thermometer registers ten degrees below.
I have already studied the mourning dove
who rests on a snowy, forking branch and preens,
as if spring has burst forth in the night.

My steaming mug invokes a string of images
that turn my daily ritual into mystery, miracle.
Who first took a dare and chewed a bitter berry?
Who dropped the bright red cherry into the fire?

Who decided to boil a bean in water?
Fifteenth century stories about coffee abound
and I get to believe any that suit my fancy.
What I like to imagine about the cup before me

is that its berries were picked by someone whistling,
happy with work that is so easily measured, rewarded.
There is also a man in a straw hat turning the berries
with a wooden rake, using his calloused hands,

drying them in the equatorial sun.
The seaman who sails with pallets of burlap bags
loves the leisurely pace across the water,
the adventure of storms, and admits with glee,

that too much money gets spent upon reaching shore.
The roaster learned his craft from his father,
and his father learned the art from his father.
This ebony pool affirms that I am blessed,

that I am connected to the sun, wind, earth, ocean,
and others like me that know physical work to be
honest, rewarding to the soul, and bound to those
for whom they toil and love.

Part II

The Creation

Autumn Glory

At Dusk the Grass Shimmered

I stepped outside and had to look closer.
The grass was sparkling like diamonds
in the waning light.

The shimmering was thousands of winged insects.
They were climbing out of a thousand holes in the ground
and taking flight,

hovering excitedly over the sandy mound
from where they had just emerged.

Termites?
Infestation for sure.
Research needed…

Oh. Orgy of ants!
When conditions are perfect,
winged sexual males and females
take flight in order to mate.

Egg-laying queens play hard-to-get,
traveling until only the fittest of males reach them,
and, in mid-air,
the males explode their genitals into the queens.

The males die soon thereafter,
their lifespan measured in days.

After the shimmering spectacle,
survivors lose their wings
and live their lives underground.

It is not the romance, secrecy or drama
that finally captures the imagination,
it is the intelligent design.

Everything that needed doing was accomplished,
and done in community;
each member using the gifts given.

Distant Loons

Abracadabra. You appear.
I count eighteen of you.

I want to shout, Stay!
I long to hear your lonely wails,
your tremolos and yodels,
your loon hoots, loon hoots,
prima donnas of the North.

You dive for food, return,
and fan your broad wings
like judges flaunting their robes.

Paddle closer. Come this way.
They say that you change your call
on each lake that you visit,
magically reinventing yourself
again and again.

Come closer still.
Are you loons after all?
I'm not sure.

You cluster, paddling and turning
like a synchronized swim team.
You've got the jim-jams too,
pacing like runners before the gun.

I sense that you cannot stay.
None of you can fight
the pull of jack pine and pristine water.

Do you have an alpha
or is someone counting votes?

Suddenly, you sprint on the surface
from crack and smoke,
and then...

Aloft!

Oh!
My mistake.
You're just a bunch of old coots.

I Do Not Lie

You must believe me when I say,
that I do not lie.

In camouflage,
I watched
as forty-two doe

silently walked past
my hunting spot.
Each nose to the rump ahead.

Struck by amazement. Frozen.
Breathing shallow.
I never laid hand to bow.

Who was I
to ruin such a parade?

It's 3:00 pm Sunday

but it's more like Friday night downtown.
Everyone's cruising.

Two geese launch from the pond
honking like runaway cars—
Get out of the way!

A muskrat paddles toward shore,
painting a yawning wake as he goes.
Buffleheads and grebes dive
and pop up like jack-in-the-boxes.

Swallows circle, flit, dive and bounce up
as they feed. They refuse to hold still
to be counted.

A pair of swans paddle stately near shore.
Red-winged blackbirds sail from tree
to shoreline to peck at the grass.

A half-dozen grackles trade trees.
Sparrows shift directions in unison.
A mallard hen paddles to keep her rump
in the air as she feeds.

The spectacle is an orchestra playing the coda.

It's the water…
All of this because of life-giving water.
May the heavens be praised.

The price for this performance?
It was free!

When I hear the water sizzle
on the shower floor,
and listen to the white noise
of the kitchen faucet,

I shall think—Life.

Intelligent Design

It was a sole mourning dove,
with its half-dozen focused moves,
that spoke so clearly to me
of intelligent design.

It waddled on the sidewalk,
then grabbed a twig from the mulch,
and, as best as I could tell,
examined its many properties.

It was so particular,
like friends who grill the waiter
prior to ordering.

Off it flew with its prize,
most likely to build a nest,
but maybe a Frank Lloyd Wright.

I couldn't help but look
past the trees and into the heavens,
then into the womb of darkness,

where a globe of brooding neurons
fired at the speed of light.

Low Snow Tide

It starts first
beneath the evergreens
with olive-green rings,

then south-facing slopes
that spread streaks of hope,

then wind-swept patches.
Finally, man-made piles,
tall as a horse,

receding without drama,
(unlike the Bay of Fundy
or the waters of Mont-Saint-Michel)

rather like the shuffle of old men,
slowly, silently,
until all that is left, is its memory.

Kairos Time

The morning sun floods our deck
and begins to push against the coolness.
Our coffee mugs still steam.

Bees are crawling on the window
and another circles close by.
Recent repairs destroyed their nest
and it's time to start anew.

Bees. Amazing creatures.
Communal roles,
benevolent pollinators,
thousands of wing strokes a minute.

Navigation using the sun.
Out in the day. In at night.
There is no Central or Mountain Time.
There is only sun and moon time.

Time to reflect.
Time to begin anew.
There is only Kairos time.

Blazing Tree

It is not enough for me
to see you from afar,
as I stumble for words,
as if words would suffice...

In earnest, I approach
as my clothes record my path.

Into your ringed story I dive,
swimming through chapters and
chapters of psalms,
where first it is written,
"In the beginning..."

Suddenly, I sense
that I have been sought.
"There is no you.
There is no I.
There is only union."

Back through the pages,
to an unaware world,
from habit is said, "I come."

Dazed from the live encounter.
Knowing, but further mute.

Curly Willow

They finally came
and trimmed your limbs,
culling weak from strong.

And now you are
a sheep after shearing,
standing there embarrassed,

with bright scars
dotting your dark skin.
But green you are still,

faithfully deflecting
the fire in the west.
So much better,

than not being at all.
Live!
We treasure your presence.

Fading Circles

If your hair is white or gray,
do you remember, in your youth,

seeing dogs circle and circle
before laying down?

Four dog-generations later,
the circling has been curtailed.

Remember being told
that the circling was

the wild of the dog
making a place in the tall grass?

Are we or our creatures better off
for having taken the wolf out of the dog?

Ritual

Having floated
to the north end of the pond,
on corduroy waves,

the mute swans
command their huge muscles
into action.

The first half dozen strokes
create white explosions
on the surface

as their necks stretch
for the southern shore.
So much energy flung

as to make one think, Caracas?
But they touch down
near the spent cat tails.

They must do this
out of delight,
the joy of being alive,

piercing the air and water
with white light
because they can.

Hawk

I saw that the easterly currents
had raised the neck feathers
of the broad-winged hawk,
while he surveyed his domain
from atop the weeping willow.

What had distracted me?
I don't recall.
Looking back to the hawk,
I saw that he was gone.

Then something new
caught my eye—
a perfect circle on the grass
of feathers.

I had missed the streaking dagger
that had made the world
grow quiet.

But soon, the songbirds
could wait no longer
and began to sing from swaying limbs.

Then the cardinal and finches moved about,
painting the world
with themselves.

The Whale's Revenge

Our captain said
that we were being given
a rare treat.

We had found a mother whale
and her calf.

I kept the camera running,
recording the experience
to enjoy, over and over, back home.

The excursion finished,
we headed for a restaurant.
As we waited for our food

the table undulated
up and down, side to side,
as if it were on a boat.

A feeling of disease swept over me.
Then I realized
that it must be a spell

cast by the mother whale,
resenting its reduction
to a one-inch square.

Slow Motion

Having first shoveled a path,
now the feeder is full.

And we become conscious
of many lives

gorging out of necessity
and joy,

and how we move
in slow motion,

so as not to startle
tiny, wild things.

Tulip

for J

I got Tulip when I was three-years-old.
And now I'm eight.

So, let's see...
so that makes Tulip five-years-old.

Daddy said, that we bought her
for twenty-seven cents.

Tulip came home in a plastic bag
filled with water.

When I got up the next morning,
I could tell that Tulip had grown.

She's big now.
Probably four centimeters.

She's probably six fish-feet long.
You know, like dog years, fish-feet...

I don't want Tulip to die.
She's part of the family.

When the Young Robin

became trapped inside,
we opened doors and windows,
yet it remained.

It knew only to fly upward,
grazing the ceiling and walls
within inches of openings.

Salvation is always
the untested path,
the looming door,

the reluctant release,
the frightfully new,
the delayed humbling,

the calm after panic,
the fearless act,
the last resort.

Since You Are Not Mine

I shall not name you.
Rather, I will bow
in grateful reverence,
oh waters
from the source,
and the songs
along your surface.

In Early Spring

Two crows
against the snow—
a colon:
that precedes
the list of feathers
heading north
toward our place.

Part III

Laughing Out Loud

Vino Rosso o Blanco?

High-Brow Bird

A year before we sold our parrot, Buddy,
we sent him off to Spain
in order to learn Spanish,
since bi-lingual birds fetch a good price.
Besides, it would be classy.

Upon Buddy's return,
we introduced him to Hispanic friends
who began to laugh until tears covered their faces
and the ladies crossed their legs.

"So what did he say?" we asked excitedly.

Through his handkerchief,
Juan translated in short gulps,
"Dammit! Dammit! Shut the screen door!"

We should have sent Buddy to France.

Scribe

Rumi never wrote a word of poetry.

It fell to his faithful companion, Hussam,
to capture what Rumi said,
as Rumi spun among the great columns.

Can you see Rumi spin,
his skirt blossoming out,
his arms stretched upward?

Poor Hussam. Can you see him?
More flushed than the master
and just beginning to sputter.

"Oh camel shit. Here we go again…"
Writing faster than any man
has ever written, while yelling,

"More ink! More parchment!
Allah, have mercy! Allah, have mercy!
Will *somebody help me!?"*

all while the mystic whirled,
oblivious to the chaos,
while he in Paradise.

Have a Little Chat

Go in secret to a quiet place
and have a little chat with your body.

You might start high.
For example, you could talk to your tongue.
After all, you've been insensitive.

You've burned it,
bit it, wagged it too much,
drowned, tied and forked it,

chilied 'n peppered it,
thickened it with drink,
and French-kissed some frogs (Eew!)

What do you say, to any body part?
Well, at least three things.

Say, "How are you?" Then listen.
Don't expect great oratory from, say, your buttocks,
but do expect a response.

If it's true, say, "I appreciate you.
I can't imagine living without you."
Then listen.

Maybe the part's voice
will be something like
Fudd, Poo Bear or Capote.

Certainly say, "Thank you," and mean it.
Realize all of the years of service X has provided!

Don't stop with your head.
Can you imagine
all the mischief further down?

Don't talk to a gall bladder
that's been removed,
unless you believe in ghosts.

If, in your chat,
there has only been silence:

1. You have no faith in this religion, or
2. You are getting the silent treatment.
You've got some relationships to mend.

The Score

The idea of Jesus
took little thought for God.
"Got to be in my image
like all other humans,
but, most certainly cannot be a god.
Can no more be my son
than any other human, except—
he will be 'plugged in,' he 'gets it.'
He knows what's important."

The whole point of Jesus
is to demonstrate what any human can do—
feed the poor, heal the sick,
comfort the prisoner...

So Jesus lives his life with abandon
and people start sayin,'
"Wow, he's good. He's God.
He's the frickin' Messiah!"
which, conveniently, takes them off the hook.

Feed the poor? Nah. That's God's job.
Prisoners? Let them rot.
Heal the sick? Impossible. Can't be done.

We can imagine that God was frustrated.
"Jesus H. Christ, people!
Really!? THAT's your reaction!?"

Tie game.
God 1. Humans 1.

Grounded

Through the ages,
absent-minded birds

misplaced their body parts,
eventually becoming,

to their great surprise,
light enough to fly.

With my hair gone,
and my teeth beside the bed,

why does all my flapping fail?

Poor Man

I once saw a man
who was standing on a corner
holding a sign.

I saw that he was terribly impoverished,
for the sign read,
"Will work for stanzas."

Status Concerns

We keep asking,

Am I a BIG FISH
in a little pond?

Am I a little fish
in a BIG POND?

when all we have to do
is swim to the end of the pool

while watching for sharks.

Moving a House

You've heard the good advice before:
"Keep your eye on the ball."
But, life seems to be more like a juggler
with five balls in motion.
Take it all in. All of it…

Fred stepped out of his role
as a pharmacist to move a house,
just the way his father
and Uncle Charlie had done for a living,
when Fred was a boy.

Fred took off his white coat
and put on a layer of dirt,
droppings, and creosote
from the crawl space,
dragging those huge timbers
and house-jacks with muscles
he hadn't used in years.

But that was days ago.
Today is moving day.

Fred had picked up idle men
from in front of the Seven-Eleven.
No one had experience,
but he explained each man's job.

It was left to Henry, a wisp of a man,
to handle the long pole
used to lift wires over the peak
as the house crawled down the street.

Fred started the engine to the ancient truck,
with its dull paint and swollen bumpers.

It couldn't have a muffler.
It rumbled like thunder overhead.

Fred stretched his arm out the window,
signaling forward motion.
With the pedal to the floor,
the truck belched black smoke.

The house creaked and the truck roared
as both inched forward.
The jumbo jet's wheels came off the asphalt!
The Oshkosh was almost airborne!

Fred eased off the pedal
to land the red giant back on earth.
Not today. Weight restrictions...

Henry, squinting skyward,
hoisted the pole and raised the wires.
The house creaked and the truck roared.
A crowd was rapidly forming,
holding ears, gaping, hugging children.

Stop! Stop! Stop! Stop!
Fred squinted and leaned out to hear.
Henry was shouting over the hood
and above the thunder
as if his life depended on it.

The big house, on the big truck?
It was on Henry's toes.

Recurring Dream

In the darkness, uninvited,
it arises from a place of pain,
this nightmare of loss,
with its deafening roar,
the earth shaking beneath my feet,
and my parent's faces
disappearing into the clouds
on a white ball of fire.
It finally dawns on me
that this horror
is more a memory than a dream,
and that I am an alien.

Part IV

Art and Music

Cars and Stripes Forever

ArtPrize Grand Rapids

In September we converge in droves.
For a few days, at least,

we will think about the value of art.
We'll sense the creativity and skill of homo sapiens.

The prize money professes that art has value.
ArtPrize is good for artists and the community.

ArtPrize also distorts.
Bigger becomes better.

"Vote for me!" overpowers the art.
One must plant one's feet before a work,

and let the hype wither, flake and fall,
until what remains is someone's truth.

In the fine print beside a painting,
"Life is fragile. Live it by loving."

Snug Harbor Uptown Band

The song title forgotten,
the intro past,
the tenor sax man stood.

His young skin like white china,
bookworm glasses under auburn hair.
Nothing said "jazz" about him.

Oh, but the riffs and bends
wailed of passion and practice,
his craft a measured wildness.

Then the man on alto stood,
his brown fingers on the pearl keys
of his ancient horn.

They traded sixteens,
then eights,
then fours,

then a free-for-all between the two
that somehow fit perfectly together,
leaving listeners to wonder

about the veil between humans and sorcerers,
while they listened,
breathless as the players.

On Candid Camera

My father bought
an expensive camera
to capture our family
on holidays and vacations.

Sometime later
he added a telescoping lens,
to pull in wildlife and distant flowers.

Then, he began to focus
on strangers,
so far away they could not feel his stare,
catching them, as he did,
like the birds on our feeder,
so busy with their lives.

Babies with dinner-plate sunglasses.
A little girl eating a turkey leg.
Teetering oldsters holding hands.
A toddler of ebony parents
with an all-day sucker.
A tourist with three cameras
around his neck.
Teenagers with braces, kissing.

Each shot caught people
with one-of-a-kind faces,
mysteriously more beautiful
than any pageant winner.

Tall Ships*

The fleet of tall ships,
with their alabaster masts,
stands fast in a sea of waving grass.

So regal, they are not exiled
to distant shores.

The spread between their arms
is the space between the notes —
Wind. Music. Wind.

Wind? It is free.
It goes where it wills,
but it is drawn to royalty,
the honor to serve.

Look closely.
In the alabaster,
see the minds, hands and dreams
of decent men and women,
who softly sing,

"Leave it in the ground.
It has slept for millions of years.
Let it sleep."

Look closer still.
In the alabaster,
see the silent prairie schooners
cross the rolling seas.

* Wind turbines

Dear Vincent

It is a shame
that those around you
lacked the sensibility
to buy a work of yours,
maybe more.

Suns, stars, street scenes,
schoolboys, still-lifes,
cypresses, self-portraits.

Maybe they could have saved
your ear, your life.

How easy it is to see
that such a tumultuous soul
resorts to painting circles of grief.

Round and round they go,
like someone's finger
signaling — crazy.

How easy it is to see
that one solitary, sold painting
could not save you

from the bullet
you shot into your chest
while behind the dung heap,
so unlike your sunflowers.

The Plan

Just the other day
I came across God's plan,
scribbled on a napkin in Denny's.

Heavens...
Earth...
Waters...
Light...
Fauna...
Beasts...
   maybe humans...

To make everything priceless,
all living things must die.

Beginning looks complete.
Nothing left to do but love.

What is Art?

What would we do
with a large, dead fish?
The fish mongers
of Pike Place Fish Market
seem unconcerned

at our reluctance to buy.
The other tourists,
who are snapping pictures
of the fish toss,
aren't buying either.

We exit the market
to explore some of Seattle.
Soon, the smaller structures
give way to tall buildings
with reflective sides

of silver and gold.
A low drone is coming
from Ellis Bay.
It grows louder and louder
and louder still,

until it is felt on our skin!
Is this the end of the world?
A fighter jet screams past,
its thunder ricochets between the buildings.
Its image flashes

on the mirrored walls.
We plug our ears, spin, and gape.
We look for meaning on our faces.

the lion runs into the clouds.
The roar recedes.

Was that art?

Image in motion, with sound,
for a few seconds only?

Could anything be more dramatic? Valuable?
Can anything so deadly be called art?

On the Day of my Downfall

wiry Miss Campbell,
dressed in black
and fiddling with her collar,
was at the front of the class
holding up student art.

When she got to the painting
that was no Monet,
I just couldn't shake my head
up and down, up and down,
any longer.

I was fed up with being
a mindless puppet,
joining the other kids
in a nasally "Yes, Miss Campbell."

So, on the day of my downfall,
I told the truth.

Having turned off my
I-will-please-you grin,
and having become a soldier at Grant's tomb,
she called on me,
(kind of how a lion talks to an antelope).

"Don't you like this painting?"
I had to say no,
even though all those stares
made my ears burn.

I was caught in a conundrum—
show respect versus tell the truth.

I didn't know yet that
compliance and truth rarely hold hands.

Really. The painting looked like
a seventh-grader had done it.

Well. I couldn't spell irony at the time,
but I could feel it like a vise on my head
as I sulked over the red and cream tiles,
past the dark green lockers
and the shiny wall blocks,
moving away from the "bad kids"
doing the tango just outside their classroom doors,
all the way to that oak bench.
That oak bench.

On the day of my downfall,
having returned to my district as a teacher,
I just couldn't shake my head
up and down, up and down, any longer.
I was fed up with being a mindless puppet,
so I told the truth.

But the trip to the principal's office was much shorter.
I was already in it.

Part V

Inner Work

Ready and Waiting

Ani Ma'amin

Etty Hillesum,
you inspire me still,
having read your
letters to God,

the ones you threw
out the slits
of the cattle car
as you left for the camp.

Along with others,
you had to stand,
packed too tightly,
yet, singing Ani Ma'amin.

Oh, how those words,
Ani Ma'amin,
fill me still.

Only now have I learned
that you also sang as you entered
the gas chamber.

Ani Ma'amin—
"I believe that God will come,
even though He may tarry."

You only stopped singing
when the gas stole your song.

You, faithfully waiting,
finally, coming to God.

Declaration

You are hereby given permission
to feel the pain of living —

to ponder it
while in the wild fields,

to accept it
like spring showers,

to reflect it
in the eyes of a friend,

and to let it sink
to the bottom of your life,

where the rubies
and diamonds lie.

Do Not Cling

Shape shift or fly.
Nothing is static.

There is only change.
Things either fall to the earth
or rise into the sky.

There is only change.
Wheat to blood.
Stream to deer.
Stone to flower.
Ice to bear.
River to land.
Mouse to owl.
Leaf to woman.
Ooze to Monarch.

Do not cling.
Nothing is static.

There is only change.
Shape shift or fly.

Failure

What I have learned
from success

has perched
on my shoulder,
then flown away
at first chance.

What I have learned
from failure
has sought marrow,

and grew
the most beautiful
of flowers.

I am fond
of the rush
that streams from success.

Oh, but
the triumph, the learning,
that follows a failure…

So much sweeter, by far.

Between States

Was I awake at the time?
Had I been dreaming?
Or was I in the soft

and milky bridge
between the two,
when the great hand

went through my chest,
grabbed my spine
and shook it powerfully,

leaving me
with an unmistakable feeling
that I had been chosen,

that I had been called.
For what, you ask?
That is the rub.

Naming Injury

We cannot escape the blade
wielded by another.

Injury does not care
if we were ambushed or forewarned.

The sting summons questions.
Do I retaliate?

Should I be "the better person?"
What is behind all this pain?

Am I a victim?
What shall I name this injury?

Every blade is wielded
by someone who is afraid.

Name your injury "Fear."
Is it not difficult to hate

someone who is afraid?
Giving your pain this face

helps compassion and forgiveness flow.
The hurt begins to evaporate.

The cell door opens.
You are free.

Paradox

What is paradox, you ask?

Well, it's grabbing a jar lid
with all your might,
so as to open the jar,

but learning it's fast
from your tight grip.

Hidden Love

I must hide
how fiercely I love.

Those who consider themselves distant
would not understand.

Those who have held a grudge
imagine it impossible.

And those nearby
would be taken aback.

It is not easy
to contain a ferocious love

that scratches at the door,
howling to be set free,

more potent and wild
than a sonnet or the Montague.

Mighty Thin God

If You are everywhere,
and I believe that You are,
I am inclined to think
You are stretched hair thin.

Stretched so thin
as to challenge my faith
and cause me to ponder
hunger, tsunamis, disease, rape.

Yet, here You are,
the bed on which I lay,
the restless air I breathe,
the skin in which I live.

Should I earnestly pray
for an African child in need,
You'll be the blanket of love
an emerald ocean away.

When I can't help but weep
from the horrific news of the day
Yours are the salty tears
that I feel upon my face.

When words rush to paper
from an urge I can't explain,
it must be, has to be
thin, inexplicable You.

It Is Me Again

Trying to make images of you,
in order for me to pray.
Today, you are the tip of a thorn

on a red rose bush.
Concentrated power and beauty.
Something I can grasp.

Today, you are a mountain range
snow and stone to the horizons.
Concentrated power and beauty.
Something I can see.

Today, you are waves pounding the shore,
endless energy.
Concentrated power and beauty.
something I can hear.

It is me again,
shrinking you down to my size.

Lights in the Storm

When Thomas Merton was alive,
he took a photo of a hook,
and it became a favorite of his.

While he said it was the only
known photo of God,
the hook represented something else, as well.

Responsibility.
Always being on the hook…
If not me, than who?

On my wall, a battered lighthouse
somehow endures the raging cerulean sea,
as the water grows into a mountain,
probing every block and seam,

then shape shifts to a verde python
and savagely smothers its prey.

What I like best is the man in the doorway,
dwarfed by structure and surge,
so small and vulnerable against such power.

He reminds me to be humble
and helps me define my place
in the great order.

For I wish to be small in all things
save love and reaching for a platter.

Solitude

Silence is the only language
that can hold
the mysteries of life.

Words?

Even when they intensify all that they
are into the point of a thorn,
they fall short,

proclaiming half-truths,
pointing to the moon,
yet are not the moon at all.

Worse yet, they often divide,
failing to include
and, therefore, succeeding to exclude.

Leave the street.
Close the door behind you.

Sit. Be still.
Invite the volumes to enter.

Three Simple Words

When he said them,
my watch stopped.

People froze like statues,
others like those in yellow photos.
Some reacted as if the president had died.

How could anyone take all the world's religions
and squeeze them into just three simple words,
like the Bible written on a period,
the oceans placed in a thimble,
or ten thousand clowns in a tiny car?

Surely, under scrutiny, his summary would collapse.
But he had gone and done it.
Those three words were flying about the room,
and in my head, like bats,
making my truth meter seesaw
like a runaway metronome.
Yes. No. No. Maybe. Yes. No.

"The message of the world's religions is the same—
Be not afraid."

I had this urge to call for a straw vote
and kick the phrase out the door
as an imposter, intruder.

If this was a great truth,
has the truth ever done us any good?

Be not afraid…
Of course, angels have said as much.
But the evidence at hand was thin.

The room could only hold
those three words, not a syllable more,
not a library of books,
not a monastery of monks,
not a warehouse of unsolved cases.
Just three simple words.

Be not afraid…
The phrase became my mantra over months
until it had withstood
every assault I could muster.

Like a lighthouse, those slender words
stood against the most ferocious
storms I could conjure.

Beneath the surface,
at work, at play,
we tremble.
Then, exhausted,
we sleep
until the nightmares come.

Stand in mountain pose.
Legions of witnesses press your back,
urging you to be salt and light,
counseling and proclaiming—
Be not afraid!

On the Day

my father died,
a person from "Laundry"
said that my mother's unmarked clothes
needed marking, right away.

She returned within an hour
with Ruth B. on dozens of labels.

My daughter scrounged two irons
and a pair of ironing boards.
So we ironed those god dammed labels
into my mother's clothes,
while standing by his empty bed.

I still cannot decide
if the lady from laundry
was strikingly callous
or if she'd thoughtfully
given us something to do.

On ironing-labels day,
I placed pens, glasses, a sales tax chart,
flashlight, ties, and humidifier manual
into a cardboard box,
and took Dad's life home with me.

You are not a Mistake

not an accident!
So, why are you here,
besides feasting on the world?

What are your gifts?
What are your intentions?

How shall you heal what is swollen?
Make sound what is thin?

Part VI

Leavings

Back to Nature 2

Lost

Annie,
Do you remember
the time you were lost?
We do.

We had driven you
to a dog-lover's farm,
so we could go on vacation.

One of the perks of coming home
was picking you up.
But, you were gone.

JoBeth said that the Harley
blatted so loudly
that you bolted.

She called and called
and looked and looked.
You were gone.

We rode horseback near and far— nothing.
We distributed flyers and called folks— nothing.
We parked our car in a field, doors open,—nothing.

We saw you in the pines,
but you were so spooked,
you ran, even from us.

Finally, we gave up.
We hoped you'd find a home
where the people would love you.

A few days later JoBeth called.
"Guess who's at my back door?"

You were wet, muddy and shivering.

JoBeth said, "Come tomorrow.
I'll get her all cleaned up."

You came back to us
all fluffy and smiling
(and sporting some ink).

Ours is a pretty good story,
but it must fall far short
of the one you could tell.

Mud

for C

My night
had turned into a season,
then more.

Questions mocked answers.
Way was closed.

Had I vision,
I would have guessed—mud.

Overwhelming. Relentless.

It rose over my toes,
ankles, legs, then more.

I cannot tell you
why I chose calm over panic,

silence over screams,
and, finally, surrender.

Only now do I know my error.
I had been covered in love.

Poor to Poorer

Last century, a cotton share cropper
was a slave with an elevated name;
in debt for seed and staples,
as if he were in chains.

When the tractors came,
whole families became even poorer,
"tractored off" into the hardness of the cities.

Praise be to men and mules
who return to the earth,
in accordance with The Plan.

Beware the angry grizzlies
that snatch work from human hands
and bread from a family's table.

Look about.
The grizzlies are everywhere,
sulking by barns and near the woods,
growling in the night,
"Bury me! I dare you."

Years Ago

It was the can of WD-40,
so carefully wrapped and lovingly given,
that made Rhonda stop short.

She did not hear her beau say
that WD-40 could fix anything,
nor the list of uses that followed.
She was dreaming of better days.

Rhonda thought she wanted more
than just to be loved.
She wanted status and wealth.
She wanted rich friends.

She wanted cool lemonade
served to her well-heeled guests
from under a white tent
in her sprawling front yard,
not one with junk cars sporting tree trunks
where their engines used to be.

Rhonda couldn't know, yet,
that she would become a trophy wife
who would have everything
that she had ever wanted, except being loved.

She would climb down from her pedestal,
only to be placed on a shelf.

That can of WD-40?
It could have even prevented a broken heart.

Do Not Vote

and then
go back to bed.

Do you really think
that men,

bought with the money of others,
will heal this bleeding world?

Part VII

Open Up!

Tulips: The Inside Story

Life is...

like a thousand-piece puzzle,
when you first open the box.

Who am I?
What am I to do?

Life's big questions
can cause the top to pop off
and the pieces to scatter everywhere.

You start, full of hope,
then discouragement sets in.
I'll never put this together...

Then you remember
to find the straight pieces.
You might come across a corner.

But, at some point, you walk away
and become a captive of distractions.
If you're lucky, you return and search anew.

You make a frame
and you begin to work in from that.
Small victories help you continue.

Finally, there it is—
your life.

Ordinary Day

Upon rising,
I did the harsh things first—

checking my appointments
and glancing at the clock.

Then birdsong
from a red-winged bird

broke through my cloak.
The lilacs gave off

their heavy perfume,
the trees recited sonnets

while the pond began
its blue-diamond dance.

And I paused to consider
the gift Today,

wondering if such a debt
I could ever repay.

Is That So...

The fruit of solitude
taught him

to embrace the news,
good or bad,
with, "Is that so..."

The fruit of experience
taught him

to lay aside judgment,
place everything

in his crucible,
and turn it to gold.

The Early Summer Sun

streams through the window,
as if it were Easter morning,
and onto the plant

that probably cannot be saved.
Its leaves are yellow and droop
over the edge of the pot.

There are ten "residents" in "The Terrace,"
the deceptive name given to the area
where those with dementia live.

They do not notice the staff and visitors
that walk in and out of the room.
The only sound is Barney Fife,

in high pitches,
explaining his worldview
to Mayberry's Sheriff.

There is egg on my mother's chin
from breakfast three hours ago.
The staff acts sleepy,

as if I'm the first person
to have spoken to them
since arriving four hours ago.

I am angry, discouraged.
I want to restate my non-negotiables;
one being, that my mother's face

gets wiped clean after meals.
But, I've said this too many times before.

No one here is Elijah.
Life will not surge back into these beautiful people
who sit and mostly stare.

But, I want them to water that god-dammed plant,
the one thing that could be fully alive,
the one thing that could represent so much.

From this moment forward,
I proclaim that these quiet souls
shall be called The Treasured People,

their last few words—gold.
Their last few steps—diamonds.
Their urine—citrine.
Their last coherent thoughts—rubies.

Staff,
By your care for The Treasured People,
you shall be named.

And and And

Dear Little Ones,
I know what's coming
in the schools you attend.

The politicians have hijacked your lives
and your teachers are choosing conformity
over protecting you.

Everything has been arranged
for you to be a pawn.
The rich and powerful want

your body, mind and soul,
no questions asked.
Don't resist on the outside.

Join your class in sing-song voice.
"Yes, Miss Pritchard," when asked to agree.
Take the damned test without a fuss.

But, don't give up when they herd you
into narrow corridors of thought.
Be agreeable,

then secretly blow those walls to bits.
The correct answer is not only A,
it is B and C and D and E.

When you're told they need engineers,
feel what calls to your heart and bones.
When told you have two choices,
worker ant or worker bee,

nod and know there are vacancies
for keepers of dreams.

When they ask you to bow to coal and oil,
smile and love the trees, and grasses,
and the sun and the wind.

Guard your precious life with Ands.

Grumbler

When did you go blind
to beauty?
Ignorant of grace,
you walk by doors
without knocking.
Find the uncommon door.

As for Our Tribe

As for our Tribe,
this is what we believe.

Why are we here in this darkness
if not to be of use?
If not to be used up like a candle?

We have picked mushrooms, peaches
and buried our dead.
We have poured milk for the children
and praised the stars.
We have oiled hinges
and confessed our sins.
We have watered the fields
and made our lovers shudder.
We have built skyscrapers
and filled begging bowls.
We have cast off judgments
so we could understand.
We have wailed from loss and failure
and celebrated always.
We have pulled forth the future
from our blood-red wombs.
We have felt the ground shake
when our lives met the great work.
We have let our hearts break
so they could grow larger still.
We have walked toward humbleness,
our steps crooked, but true.
We have chosen our path from the circle
where all voices were heard.
We have set our bows to symphonies
and have thanked our god.

We have harvested what we planted.
We have asked questions of the mountains
and have not wished for simple answers.
We have passed on what was given to us.
We have danced and sung for joy,
but have gone still to listen.
The sighted among us have helped the others to see.

Have we been of use?
It is not for us to say.
What we do know
is that it is never too late to be of use.

Send our cold bodies to the desert,
the place where scientists bury remains,
only to dig them up.

The scientists will say about one of us:
"Had a victim been murdered seven months ago,
he would look like this."

Another,
"Had a victim been buried 400 days ago,
she would look like this."
Murderers will be caught from the news we bring.
The grave is just a new door.

Give our cold bodies to medical schools.
We sing in unison, "Take us. Take us now!"
Unwrap the miracles that we are.
Probe our mysteries and become
beacons of hope, instruments of light.

Bury our cold bodies standing,
we, who shall smile,
beneath the reaching trees.
Oh, how blessed we are,
we who have found the shared life—
The power of consent.
Participation.
Trading needs and gifts.
The joy of feeling spent.
The peace of being used up.

We, The Tribe
completely still—
still dancing.

At the Funeral

Today, you and I
were courageous.

You sang and I played
as beautifully as we could.
We wanted every note
to be perfect.

It is a shame
that we had to steel ourselves,
so as not to fall apart,
clenching notes that could not be scattered.

We became chameleon people.
Fabricating hearts of stone,
while ours were really breaking.

When the incense filled our noses
And those gathered bid farewell,
we could finally unloose our tears.

Christmas Season

So much has been done
to receive and celebrate Him—

candles, concerts,
wreathes, wrapped gifts,

special recipes, reenactments
music and manufactured moods.

The days march forward
without pause.

Nothing can stop His birth,
all that followed

and all that it means—
except my heart.

So I wonder if I am able
to make room

for something so boundless
and misunderstood,

so powerful and mysterious,
if the trembling ghost,

who whispers "me,"
will yield and kneel.

Infinite Worlds

After God built the world,
it wasn't long before brother
was killing brother.

Eventually God turned the keys over
to Ben Franklin and Charles Manson
and you know the rest of the story.

But this world is only one possibility
of endless possibilities.
There are versions that would make Jesus

dance for joy.
Don't you wonder about other possible versions
if the keys had been kept by, say,

JFK and Phyllis Dillar
or Joan of Arc and Groucho Marx?
And what if you and I

had been given the keys?
Would Heaven be
"just up the stairs and to the right?"

Would Justice be sitting in the parlor?
And would there still be flowers?
Would they be less of delicate distractions

and more an expression of the world's essence?
And would God be so happy
as to say, "The keys? Keep 'em."

Jean Donovan (1953-1980)

Jean Donovan,
I thought of you today,
a day like any other,
but maybe I needed inspiration,
a reminder that humans

are just one breath short of angels.
You started out as an accountant,
but God kept nudging and pestering.
Like Moses, you resisted and argued,
"Why are you doing this to me?

Why can't I just be your little suburban housewife?"
all the while walking toward God.
Before they dumped you in a shallow grave,
the death squad raped you and shot you dead.
I see now that you were a powerful threat, like Jesus,

that had to be brought low and killed.
Though not its purpose at all,
Love can't help but shame oppressors
and rattle the hollowness of their hearts.
After the Archbishop was killed

and the Peace Corps workers left,
you considered your own safety.
But, the little tan children,
orphaned, homeless, hungry, terrified,
who would wipe their tears?

Who would bury their parents?
Who would bind the wounds of peasants
caught in the crossfire of paper men gone mad?

Jean Donovan, your witness gives me hope.
In it I see that God, through the millennia,
continues to call and intercede,
shaping mere humans into sacred hosts of communion—
chosen, blessed, broken,
offered, taken, eaten.

VIII

Dark Times

Help Wanted

Hubris Hell

The incident was minor and long ago.
By this time,
the feuding parties

had polished their positions
and spent more on lawyers
than the plaintiff had asked for relief.

At a pretrial meeting
the defendants kept apologizing,
but it wasn't enough.

The plaintiff wanted the defendants
to say that the incident happened
just as he said it had.

Anything else was a lie.
In good conscience, they could not.
Their perspective was different.

The fierce reality
was that the pompous man
was living in a world bounded by his skin.

The opinions of others didn't matter.
The others didn't matter.
His truth was the only truth.
His world was the only world that mattered.

So the plaintiff proudly announced,
that, since they couldn't agree,
they would have to go to court.
He wanted justice.

The lawyers smiled
and the hostages sagged,
all thanks to the incredibly ugly,
shrinking man.

On the Coast of France

I have already wept on the manicured lawn,
beside the white crosses above Omaha Beach.

In the uneasy silence,
I wait for the dead to say

that they have no regrets,
that freedom exacted a price they were willing to pay.

Instead, my friend looks about and whispers—
what a waste.

If we could rewind time,
to save these lives, and many others,

how far back would we have to go?
Say Cain and Able, if you must.

Finally the silence speaks.
"I am here to distract you from the violence, pain,
and broken dreams."

The lessons arrive like waves on the shore.
They say over and over,

Distrust men who cannot regard strangers
as equals and as brothers.

Distrust men who believe that violence is the solution
when it is really the problem.

Until peace reigns in the hearts of all men,
weep with me.

Requiems

While symphonies stand as monuments
to human creativity,

it is the inspired requiem
that eclipses those works,

drawing from the depths
that only sorrow can reach

and the keening
of a grieving God.

Worried

I messaged you. I called your cell.
You did not answer.

The ground began to tremble
and my mind unraveled.

Drowning in doubt,
I thought the worst.

Had the sirens
drawn you to the rocks?

Had Procrutus
forced you to bed?

Had Ares
spent his mood on you?

Oh, most loved,
if the worst has befallen you,
be Phoenix.

While You Were Dying

I would repeat,
from time-to-time,
words that I thought would comfort.

It's okay.
Everything is done that needs doing.
Everything's alright. Just let go.

Today, I am clinging
to my own little life,
wondering if I had spoken true to you.

In the desperate darkness,
that held us both,
would I not have said the truest of truths?

You There, Crying

I can see
that your heart is broken
by the shards around your feet.

Wail into your pillow.
No one leaves here
with their heart unscathed:

The sudden death…
The surprise betrayal…
The savage end…
The searing judgment…
A longing unrealized…
A failed plan…

Howl and rent your shirt.
Let the hurt sink in.

Those shards are epidermis
cast off when your heart grew larger,

ever more ready for love,
more ready for life.

Let Us Do It for You

We hear where 'er we go,
"You know so very little,
it's us that really know."

Unless you're very careful,
and see the price you'll pay,
they'll steal your will and muscle
and your brain will soon decay.

You shouldn't give yourself away.
You must not fall asleep.
The tipping point approaches.
Are you a shepherd or a sheep?

Stop Bitching!

How would you
like to be a caveman,
with a toothache,
and the nearest dentist
60 millennia away?

When You Are Down

When you are down,
ride the hurt to the bottom
until only a rope will help

and thank God
that there's no rope in the house.
For time will help you heal

and, most likely,
all of creation is working
to set things right.

Aint no human gonna
leave this good earth
without something for which to howl.

Don't waste your energy guessing
who has done you in.
If you can, dance.

Dance, if you can.
Dance and howl to end the guessing.
Leave the music to Mystery.

When I Failed

to comfort my brother,
Dad came up the stairs
and let us get out of bed.

We gathered at the window
and waited for the veins of light
being chased by thunder.

Dad's voice was calm
as he kept talking to my brother,
that there was nothing to worry about.

See? Lightening,
and then thunder…
We are still okay, aren't we?

I watched their faces,
faintly lit by the street light,
their skin all mottled

from raindrops on the window,
then bleached by crooked fingers
that ran ahead of the thunder.

They looked into the night sky
as I looked at them,
my father comforting my brother.

The two of us,
with horses on our pajamas,
didn't become men that night,

but both of us knew
that we had a good man as a guide.

The Angels Have Left

Neighbors are suggesting
that the angels are gone,
maybe for good.

Two months ago
they left singing Hallelujah! Hallelujah!
but they haven't been seen since.

We are beginning to believe
that we can no longer live by sight.

That, in the future,
we shall have to live by faith.

Part IX

About God

Majestic Beauty

God is...

God is the Mysterious Self,
acting in the world,
while you read these words.

God will forever create,
whether there are humans to sense it,
or not.

God's Work

If we are to be about God's work,
then, exactly, what is that?

We already know,
but we bury our awareness in the service of "me."

God's work is the common good—

where I can no longer be king of my castle
while others are homeless,

consume feasts
while others starve,

enjoy my success
while others are jobless,

hoard in closets
what's needed in the streets,

and pick leaders
that favor my comfort.

Having gone west,
I must now go east,

deciding that the common good is the highest good,
and that it is also good for me.

From the First Day

We should not be surprised
that logs burn brightly,
that the distant stars

are radiant suns,
that diamonds and waters
reflect and sparkle,

that sand turns to glass
so light can pass through,
that the cold moon

turns night into day,
that whales and black crude
can brighten a room,

that volcanic mountains
are glowing fountains,
that frigid realms shimmer

and fireflies pulse,
that sandworms and plankton
glow in the dark.

For is this not the world
made by the God of Light?

It is Impossible to Imagine

how many times
the words of a medieval monk

have been passed on
from generation to generation.

Finally arriving today
are the words of Father Lawrence.

"We are like trees in winter,
stripped bare with nothing to offer,

yet, we are loved by God.
There are times in our lives

when all we can offer is our shadow,
as we stand stiff and empty-handed."

But Father Lawrence might have continued.
We are created in the image of God,

sculptor of the world,
omnipotent,

lover of all creation,
grand god of patience,

wondering when we will finally "get it,"
and bring forth

a bountiful harvest
of equality and peace.

It's Really Quite Simple

The trappings of religion
are, well, traps.

So caught up in rules,
tongue twisters and begats,

our faith falters
from shalls and confusion.

It's really quite simple.

Love yourself, then your neighbor.
Embrace your shadow.

Judge not.
Discover your gifts and use them.

Be present to others.
Give yourself away.

Melted

As the cancer inside simmers,
I know what I fear most—

that you won't let me go,
that I can't let you go,

that I will be called
while we are locked

in an embrace of give and take,
needing and receiving what the other has,

our backs to the God
who would heal.

Don't We Know

that God is Love?
Don't we know
that God is Mystery?

Don't we know
God is Active Creator?
Anything else is religion.

Pursuit

Oh, how long
since you knocked me off my feet

and put the blue flame in me?
Like always, there is a volcano coming.

I can feel it inside,
a wobbling pan before the hiss,

a pregnant mountain before the blood,
building toward a fervent scream.

I know you are here.
Have mercy! Speak!

Climb Down

Climb down. Climb down.
Climb down now.

Rarified air has made you confused.

Having clawed over so many backs,
you still take credit for the work of others,
crowing but unable to fly,
hoarding wealth that could feed the starving.

You have misread the stars,
jumping over jagged roots
grown for your salvation.

The way to God and your fellow man is down.
It has always been this way.
It shall always be.

Climb down your one-legged ladder.
Climb down. Climb down.
Climb down now.

Part X

In the Midst of Family

Let Me Up!

The Joy of Retelling

My father used to tell
of how terribly cold
his hands would become,
as if thrust into fire,

when picking the white celery
from the frozen muck,
in the black of early morning.

I was always caught up in this tale,
and others,

not by his telling,
but by his pure joy of recollection.

Praise be to the past!
Amen.

Memory Fails

Why didn't I write them all down,
the stories that were told to me,
the ones that explain who I am,
but failed to stay?

Now, there are only feathers
of my lineage to grab in the wind,
the places, dates and names
are sand through an hour glass.

But a few fragments remain:
a family member, a man,
walking hundreds of miles
to reach home from the war,

standing at the gate,
with a shotgun on his shoulder.
The women, with flushed cheeks,

snapping beans and hanging wash,
stare in disbelief,
then scream and run with abandon.

But other shards are less revered:
Charlie liked his beer
and the gossip at the union hall.

In the Mirror

I keep waiting to see my father stare back at me
as I search the mirror for a likeness.

I am evidence
that dominance is relentless.

Mamma Boy hair.
Mamma Boy eyes.

I might have Dad's nose,
but he broke it while playing football.

He reset it himself after the game.
Not very well.
I never saw it otherwise.

Do I throw my left leg out
when I walk?

I can still see that gait
that seemed to imply that he loved life.

Finally, I do see something —
the joy gene.

Simplicity

The romance is gone
from poverty.

The romance is gone
from wealth.

I must return to the discipline
and good sense of an earlier day —

the wisdom to know
what is enough.

I long to hear
my great grandmother say,

On your bread,
you may have jam or butter,
not both.

The Formal Meeting

The only family meeting
ever called to order
in the most grim of tones,
left an indelible mark.

I sat cross-legged on the floor
near my brother.
Dad was on the couch
his face drained of life.

Mom was in a heap
in the stuffed, swivel chair,
grasping a rumpled Kleenex
with both hands.

Who died?
Just tell me.

Mom couldn't take it anymore;
the washing, the meals
the housework, the bookkeeping
running for repair parts, church circle
PTO, band boosters

I don't remember
how long and hard
I tried to make less work
and to faithfully do chores.

But I remember my promise,
said so fervently to myself,
the words could have etched stone,
Mom, I will never make you cry again.

Without Training Wheels

His mammoth hand on the seat,
Dad gave me a mighty shove,

and then bellowed from behind,
Pedal! Keep going!

Scared.
Elated.
Wobbling.

I learned that the grass was my foe,
rising up as it did,

between the two tracks
and the sides of the drive.

No Spanking Please

Somewhere
there must be a place
where a woman is giving birth

to the sounds of lush strings,
light neither dark nor bright,
and where the voices are hushed.

If the child needs help
with its first breath,
those gathered resort to psalms.

With such a beginning to life,
so laden with meaning,
might the world tip toward peace?

Snowman

Out in the snow
with the girls,

I couldn't recall
when I had last

made a snowman.
Probably fifty years or so.

I made three cannonballs
from the sharp crystals.

I told the girls
to roll theirs

on the snow in the sun.
I watched the youngest

lose interest.
I heard the eldest

call her out.
If I chose to be faithful,

he would be fine, indeed.
As my ball kept growing,

old memories faded,
in preference to glee.

In the Attic

Was it a barn or a garage?
I do recall that its sides
were patterned blocks
and that it had a gambrel roof.

It must have been off limits,
for when I stepped inside,
I could feel the eyes of the world
begin to stare,
as only a child can feel.

The fragrance of lilacs at the door
was replaced
with the suppressive smell
of dusty, still air.

Up the stairs, on the right,
I climbed.
When I reached the top,
I stood still.

I let my eyes adjust to the darkness
that squeezed the light
into excited bars
that struck the uneven floor.

Then I saw it—
a sea chest.
I opened the large latch
and raised the rounded top.

It was then that I saw them.
The wooden shoes.

How deeply,
and far back in time,
can a five-year-old imagine?

Across the sea, beside the canal,
I saw a man bending over,
harvesting a crop,

one, whose blood
pumped through me faster,
as I strained to see his face.

The Youngest

for M

You were born second.
and you're also the last.
Being a first,

I labor to imagine
how tough life must be,
watching another do things well,

sometimes slowed from trying,
you, who keep hearing,
"In a couple of years, you can too."

You probably don't notice
that I'm your clandestine champion,
listening to you with my whole being,

applauding any success into a triumph,
hoping with wild abandon
that joy fills your days,

you, who wear clothes
that I've seen before.
Know this secret.

I love you in a special way,
to perturb that which is,
straining to make you first, as well.

Fingers and Toes
for F

When your sister was born,
we brought you to the third floor,
to see her.

She was so new,
that your daddy was in the nursery,
counting fingers and toes.

I watched your beautiful face
in the reflection
of the nursery window.

Your fascination matched mine.

Your daddy, such a clown,
held up ten fingers, twice.

But having seen your sister,
minutes before,
we already knew that she was perfect.

Earthquake

for J

I remember the day that I realized
you and I were separate people.
I had been confused when thinking
that we were one being
with two names.

We had just left the awards ceremony
where you received
the "Student of the Year" award.
Walking down the hallway,
you shared that the award
had been your goal.

The building shook with wild tremors.
I could hardly stand.
You were living a separate life,
secret keeper,
daughter of mine,
stranger.

Saying Goodbye
for J & S

At Terminal 3,
I placed your large bags on the curb,
as you both grabbed your knapsacks.

We hugged and kissed.
Our emotions seemed
the better side of neutral.

After all,
you were starting an adventure.

You thanked me for the ride
and the loan of my coat,
then, we parted.

Out on I-190,
I thought to myself,
Brazil…

Definitely not Kansas.
Definitely not Fort Wayne.
Come back to me soon.

They Won't Change Their Plans
for F

Even though Grandma Doris died today,
they'll still drive south to Tennessee
(for a funeral instead of a visit).

They'll turn east at Nashville
and head into the back country
of mobile homes and lilacs
and long stretches of white fences

that keep out people scraping to get by,
the ones that make you wonder
how they make a living at all.

The world has lost an artist
whose loose watercolors of hills,
woods, barns and mountains
cause one to dream.

The world lost a rare person
who could think original thoughts
and refused to accept sound-bite drivel.

The world lost a Democrat.
Not any old Democrat,
rather, one with justice in her bones.

Seems Grandma Doris couldn't wait to see them.
She could feel the Republicans in the Big House
getting too noisy and full of themselves.
Talking heads beware.
Heaven's going to get a new coat of paint.

Aunt Jennie Klepper

had a kind soul.
If no one beyond Mom and Dad
remembered my birthday, she would.

She had a sense of humor, wisdom,
and could pray like a preacher.
She was widowed early
and became a nanny for income.

When her families were on vacation
she would visit one of her sisters
and the other three would travel
to catch up on the news.

She would look the same each visit—
ivory hair, silver-rimmed glasses,
black, low-heeled shoes,
carrying that shiny, black "pocketbook."

I loved these hard-working women
and enjoyed their banter.

Aunt Jennie had a crush
on the father of her charges.
She said with a smirk

that she wouldn't mind
if he stirred her coffee
with his socks.

Oh how they would snicker
and refill their coffee cups,
adding cream and sugar.

I Listened to You Breathe

I listened to you breathe,
in the dead of night,
while the rattle became pronounced.

You had one final task to do
and you worked with abandon.
Somewhere in the darkness,

when both hands of the clock
pointed to a new day,
I thought of the ocean—

the thunderous rumbling
and the white noise
of the waves running to the shore

and The Deep pulling them back to itself.
In, out.
In, out.

Your waves grew still.
Your work done,
you could now become

something wonderful and mysterious all over again.
A saint.
An angel.

A heavenly host.
An ocean,
whose waves rhythmically

sought my shore,
over and over,
waves that would not stop—

surges of vinegars, acids, oils,
and my depths
pulling them in.

Done With School

For my father,
school was a shoe
that didn't fit.

"I graduated in 1937 with cap and gown
and the whole nine yards.
Boy, was I glad to be done with school."

Dad dragged me all over the state
so he could study how gravel pits
were laid out.

He bought an airplane
so he could learn how to fly.

He studied photography
and sound-recording.

He took up computers
to run his golf league.

I guess the school-shoe was too small.

Perfect Fit

for E & J

I was surprised
to experience bliss,

when my grandchildren's
tiny heads,

fit perfectly
against my neck.

Birth

Your mom and dad,
and the doctor,
were in the birthing room.

You were about to be born.

Grandma and I
were leaning on the door,
so as to hear what was happening.

Oh, how excited we were!

The doctor opened the door,
and Grandma almost fell into the room
and onto the floor!

Oh, how we laughed,
for so many reasons!

Grandchildren

Water faithfully,
but do not drench.

Fertilize,
but do not smother.

If wandering,
provide trellis.

Shelter from the wind.
Talk to them.

Watch patiently.
When they bloom,

tell them often
how wonderful they are.

Designs

Midway of mowing the lawn,
two granddaughters appeared on the drive.

Each wanted a turn
on the tractor.

I couldn't help but glance
at the straight lines of where I'd been.

While on my lap
circles were made,

and figure eights,
and designs for which there are no names.

And the last one only stopped
when there was nothing left to draw.

Bread

Flour,
water,
salt,
yeast.

While baking,
it throws off the years,
like a spring jacket, until I am five

and in my aunt's kitchen,
wound tight as a spring,
waiting for the loaves to cool.

Hands in Water
for J

I remember the day very well.
I came to your house
to see you and your tiny daughter.
She was just days old
and you were going to bathe her.

You set a small tub of warm water
on the kitchen table.
The low November sun
found its way through the window
and began covering her.

How gentle you were,
as you wet the washcloth,
wringing it slowly,
then washing her face.
This being your first child,

I was surprised at how confident
and comfortable you were.
That is when you asked
if I would like to help,
and you offered to show me how.

It wasn't long before
my hands were in
my granddaughter's bath water,
your hands beside mine,
in the waters of time.

Waving Goodbye

In the darkness of early morning,
we stand on the driveway
and watch you pull away.

We summon the energy to wave,
our arms trying to say,

We love you.
Be safe.
Have a wonderful life!

All of this effort
does not keep us from despair
over our parting.

How terribly we miss you,
even though you are still
on our street.

And then I think of Cracker Jacks,
of all things,

carmel corn and peanuts in a slender box,
with Sailor Jack and his dog Bingo
on the side.

Are there still prizes at the bottom?

In the Dining Room

...of the place
where old people go
to live out their days,

I stared at the caverns
between the bones
on the back of her hand
and could no longer doubt
what people mean
when they say, "skin and bone."

I kept thinking how a person
can fade away year after year.
Yet, even as we die,
there is something wild inside
that loves life and pushes on.

On her arm,
the lily pads asked to be rubbed.
On her head,
the lilacs and lace asked to be arranged.

There were little roots
growing from the corner of her mouth
and there was mud on her chin.
The spike rush and sedge
were growing between her toes.

She is a quiet pond
being reclaimed by the earth.

I saw something new
and yet very old—
an abandoned vein.
No blood coursing through it.

The forgotten path
ended in the shape of a star,
the one that burned so brightly
over Bethlehem.

This was all I could take in
while on my visit
in the dining room –

somewhere in the galaxy
one hundred thousand light years old.

After Thanksgiving Dinner

They are side-by-side,
next to the sink.

She washes and he dries
the large and the delicate
and, eventually, they sit and relax.

It is the silence,
nothing at all,
yet, so powerful,

that invades
their thoughts of the day
and their pretense at happiness.

Loss is a terrible thing,
but you bless your loved ones,
as they return to their lives,

then tend to your own,
no matter how fragile,
no matter how lonely.

Shrinking

Have you watched
how the world shrinks
when people grow old?

The second floor of their homes
migrate to a foreign land.

They take the basement stairs
on their bottoms.

They buy groceries from electric carts
with long-reach grabbers.

Someone takes away the car keys.
They stop walking to the mailbox.

In the end, their world becomes
the size of their bed.

This tragedy can only be reconciled
with the size their world used to be—

the Rockies turning gold at sunrise,
salmon swimming upstream,
Monet's garden,
Times Square at night,

given and received love,
one's chin sticky from peaches,
feeling connected to creation,
cradling a newborn,

most of life better than junior high,
the Vietnam Memorial,

morning glories opening,
a bee drinking its fill,

discovering that loving one's self
was less difficult than first imagined,
realizing that death is a fair ending
to a life well-lived,

that Being, just once,
was a gift that could not be cancelled
by a heart at rest
or a world as small as a bed.

Don't we know
that the shrinking continues further
until we fit through a keyhole
to another vast world?

Little Red Cars

A mother placed her little boy
in a red car on the merry-go-round.

The music changed
as the platform began to move.

His lip turned out
and his face said, "I'm scared."

As he went round and round,
his fear turned to delight.

He began to wave to his father,
and then, even to me, a stranger,

beneath the French clouds
by the sea and the Seine.

When the little red car ran out of gas,
it broke his heart.
He wanted to drive forever.

It was a little French boy
who caused me to think about life here
and across the seas and continents.

How scared we are at first,
of big doors, the night
and our mothers out-of-sight.

We go round and round
until we find our bliss,
and we don't want our little red car to stop.

Oh, how our lips turn out
as the music slows.

If only we could remember
how we drove and drove

and joyfully waived to people
with names we didn't know.

If only we could rejoice,
in having had a ticket at all.

Before Sleep

At the far end of day,
my head heavy on the pillow,

it is sometimes my custom
to whisper in the darkness,

"You are a good woman."

I soar on updrafts over the bed
for having sung the truth.

My wings counter
every nuance of current

and I can see the sun
over the mountain peaks.

Her hand
moves through the darkness,

to give a simple pat,
and I dive to receive it.

Then there is nothing left to do,
except praise the gods.

Part XI

Inner Life

Bare Necessities

Broken Troth

Of what could we be full
to cause our teachers to vanish?
Of what could we be empty
that makes our teachers mute?

The Buddhas die silent,
rather than entrust.
Unnoticed, shamans walk
from their villages.

How can we assuage
the present need —
to see our teachers into view
and hear them into speech?

Clarity

Death seems so tragic to some –
an unfathomable waste.

Yet, I know why I shall die.
I shall die for love.

When I let go, for the last time,
I will vanish from view

No longer blocking loved ones
to the sight of what matters most.

Dear Friend,

I'm going to ask you
to remember who you really are—
a living paradox.

Recall that you are a god.
Not one to whom
the Hebrews strayed.

No, the real deal.
The one who cures the sick,
feeds the poor, and walks on water.

Recall that you are human,
but shed your protective armor.
Reject your false identities and labels.

Throw off your religion
that demands you look Heavenward,
but blinds you to those in need.

Discard everything,
until you can feel
the pain of others.

With your compassion and power,
bring forth the world
straining to be born.

Thanks Be To You

If only I could thank you
for what you did,
a few years back,

in the dark,
as you were probably
heading home from work.

Her body out of balance,
my wife drove past our street
and out into the country.

How she pulled to the edge
and came to a stop,
I will never know.

You saw her
standing in the cold
beside her car.

You found her dazed
and unresponsive,
then called for help.

Bless you seventy times seven.
So much could have gone wrong,
so very much.

We know the most important thing
about you. That you are a good man.
But we don't know enough...

The oval on your jacket
only said, "Keith."

The Nightmare

The terror that rose up
in the middle of the night
was always the same.

I was flying.
I was flying and leaving behind
all those I loved.

They became smaller and smaller
the longer I flew
and the yawning distance a razor blade.

Because of it, and for other reasons,
this is why my love is breathless
from my fierce embrace.

Deep Inside is Me

Deep inside this borrowed body
is my borrowed heart,

and deep inside
my borrowed heart is me.

Writing these lines is not me.
The one who observes is me,

thinking these lines are only a river
that me decides to see.

Me is the shy wisp
who must hold a child,

defend the poor,
mourn when you are sad,

and love you most completely
with my borrowed heart.

Diabetic Low

Deep in the night,
even though asleep,
I wake and wonder

if your fitful sleep
is much more than that—
that you may have fallen

from the edge of the world.
I touch your neck.
I feel your back and drenched pajamas,

and learn you are gone.
Then the struggle begins,
coaxing you to drink juice,

whose sweetness will pull you back
into the world you've left.
Sometimes you readily drink.

Other times you resist.
Finally, the glass is empty.
We sit on the edge of the bed,

my arms around you,
waiting for the tears
and the usual questions.

"What happened? Where am I?"
Then you are back.

I have saved you—
a small thing, weighed against
how you have saved me.

DSM

A knock on the door...
Hmm. It could be the white coats...

I believe in angels.
I believe love is stronger than violence.
A woman should have been president by now.

I am happy.
I like eggplant and brussel sprouts.
I don't follow sports.

I don't watch TV.
Arguing people can both be right.
I vote in primaries.

I'm an introvert.
North is debatable.
Bullet-proof notions of God are bunk.

Prisons suck.
Schools are boring.
Politicians are spoiled children.

Arguing people can both be wrong.
Teachers deserve our respect.
I am right-handed, but left-minded.

Go away.
I am not home.

I Had a Nightmare My Love

You were gone
and there was no one to love
as fiercely as I love you.

There was no heart of goodness
that sees beauty everywhere.

No one to share discoveries
of the marvelous and the mysterious—

and I wept.

Then I woke
with you by my side

and a blanket of warmth
covered me

with a deeper love
'til now thought impossible.

Whatever We Truly Need

scoffs at what we have.

If we are full,
we must become empty.

If we are smoldering,
we must catch fire.

If we are afraid,
we must dance.

If we are high,
we must go low.

If your village is made of one-way streets,
find another town.

Everything is Sacred

Everything is sacred
and that which is not is also sacred,

but has fallen,
and must be redeemed.

The unholy
must be made whole

and holy again,
restored from the defiling hands of men.

That which is hideous
must be transformed.

That which has been torn apart
must be mended.

That which is at war
must be reconciled.

That which is dead
must be resurrected.

We shall again be comforted
by the presence of Heaven,

our shoulders rubbing
against its veil.

The Two Loves

For every love,
there are two loves.
When we fall in love,

we do not think
of the inevitable parting
that is paired with that love,

the time when our heart breaks,
and we are sure it will never heal.
If we thought of that parting,

as we rushed to the flame,
we'd pitch backwards
and retreat

to some sad and empty fortress.
But, no love is truly fulfilled
until it is severed,

and we are given the gift
of feeling, and knowing,
how deeply we were cherished,

and how radically
we gave ourselves away —
how priceless it all was.

Is this knowing
not worth the ravages
that bridge these two loves?

I do not pause to say yes.
I say most certainly yes.

It Is Hard To Say Hello

If you are the first on the dance floor,
and relish telling stories

to very large crowds,
you will not understand

how hard it is to say hello,
for us,

who take in the world,
and grow quieter still.

Corners

Your life comes
with a frame,

and its corners
you may name.

Consider carefully.
What will you choose?

Money, success, wisdom, gratitude?
Service, family, God, booze?

There are just four corners,
no more;

and not choosing is to choose.

Ladders

As we climb "the ladder of success,"

we do not see the millions of other ladders,
leaning against false hope and denial.

Millions of ladders. One person per ladder.
Lonely people on private ladders.

We've got to ditch the metaphor.

Better to see life as all of us on one ship—
all of us working and playing together,

breaking bread around a table,
crying salty tears, from time to time,

everyone raising the sea
that carries us all.

Very Bad News

When you discover
very bad news about yourself, Rejoice.

Light a candle. Dance.
Shout Alleluia,

for this is very good news.
The world has become a better place.

Ask this friend to stay.
Before long, you will see your friend in others

and you will refuse to judge.
And, by doing nothing,

the world will have become a better place.
Then wish for more very bad news.

Living Like a Wind

I know I've left you wondering
if I care for you at all,

that what seemed so solid before
may have fallen from your grasp.

It is not so.
I hold you still, while you live in disbelief.

You see,
I am a helpless wind.

I am blown west. I am blown east.
I'm forced to rage. I'm made to tease.

I am caught up within my days.
What else is the wind to do?

Yet, when I finally come to rest,
in front of me is your face.

Untitled

If I tried to write a poem
that would end all poems,
I think I would sit down,
in front of that white field,
and just hum what is in my heart.

Jack H. Bender – Non-fiction Author and Poet

Jack Bender has eclectic tastes and a variety of life and work experiences: US Army officer, prison music teacher, cashier, laborer, salesperson, DJ, computer programmer, musician, heavy equipment operator and public school teacher. His writing is based on the theme of personal and communal transformation through living intentionally.

He holds a Bachelor of Music Education from Central Michigan University and a Specialist in Educational Leadership from Western Michigan University.

Jack maintains his interest in conflict resolution and commitment to reducing poverty through his writing and speaking. He also enjoys arranging brass music and motorcycling in his free time. He is married to watercolor artist Cindy Bender. They live and work in Zeeland, Michigan.

All three of his books, *Disregarded, Moonflower* and *Three Simple Words,* can be found on Amazon.com or by contacting him at jhbender99@gmail.com.

Rumors that he is The Phantom Tuba Player cannot be confirmed.

Cindy M. Bender – Artist

   Cindy Bender began painting with watercolors after retiring from 23 years of teaching elementary students. She read and experimented, attended workshops and paints at the Holland Area Arts Council with a group of artists. Painting has taught her to look at the world differently—becoming more aware of color, shadow, light and texture. She is a strong believer in the importance of art in the life of every person!

   She has been in art competitions and exhibits including the Michigan Watercolor Society, Muskegon Regional, First Church spiritual show in Grand Rapids, Grand Haven winter show, the Holland Regional and MI Arts shows. Her watercolors can be found at Studio 2 in Montague, Michigan Grand Expressions in Grand Rapids and in The Red Chair Gallery and Studio in Zeeland. Cindy Bender graduated from Central Michigan University with an English major and music minor and earned her Master's in Elementary Education from Western Michigan University. She loves to sing and was a member of the Grand Rapids Symphony Chorus for 27 years. Currently, she is a member of the St. Francis de Sales church choir and is also a cantor there. She enjoys motorcycling and has fun helping in her grandchildren's classrooms.

   To contact Cindy, visit www.cindymbender.com.

Made in the USA
Middletown, DE
23 May 2016